ANCHOR BOOKS

CELEBRATIONS IN VERSE FROM THE EAST

Edited by

Sarah Andrew

First published in Great Britain in 2001 by
ANCHOR BOOKS
Remus House,
Coltsfoot Drive,
Peterborough, PE2 9JX
Telephone (01733) 898102

HB ISBN 1 85930 981 X
SB ISBN 1 85930 986 0

FOREWORD

For many of us the medium of poetry offers us a voice - a voice to speak out and let others know what we feel, think and desire. It is the vital bridge of communication that lets us share our innermost thoughts and messages on life to people who may need that vital surge of poetic inspiration.

Each of the chosen poems have been specifically favoured from a large selection of entries sent. As always, editing proved to be a difficult task and as the editor, the final selection was mine.

Celebrations In Verse From The East is a unique collection of poetry and verse written in a variety of styles and themes, brought to us from many of today's modern and traditional writers, who reside in this area. The poems are easy to relate to and encouraging to read, offering engaging entertainment to their reader.

This delightful collection is sure to win your heart, making it a companion for life and perhaps even earning that favourite little spot upon your bookshelf.

Sarah Andrew
Editor

CONTENTS

A SAILOR'S SPRING

Open the hatch and peer within,
Everything is dark and dim.
A fusty smell greets the nose,
Must make sure that goes.
Unfurl the sails and let them blow,
Polish the brass work down below.
Scrub the deck and varnish the wood,
Fit that brand new spray hood.
Check the engine and change the oil,
Make sure the carpet not to spoil!
Charge the battery, check all ropes and stays,
Can't have any of those giving way.
Pump the bilges till they're dry,
Fill the fresh water tank up high.
Stock the cupboards with tins of food,
Don't forget the cans of booze.
Scrape the bottom and anti-foul,
Then let out a great big howl!
We *are* ready at last and the tide is high,
It's time to say to the shore goodbye.

Mary Antcliffe

MY DREAM

Last night as I lay sleeping I had the strangest dream,
I saw a little cottage beside a rippling stream,
There were flowers in the garden and roses round the door,
A picture of serenity that filled my soul with awe.

I walked the winding pathway beneath the shady trees,
I heard the songbirds singing and felt the gentle breeze.
Then as I raised my hand to knock the door swung open wide,
A soft voice bid me enter and so I stepped inside.

There seated in a rocking chair was a lady old and grey,
Her wrinkled face was smiling as she turned and looked my way.
She handed me a picture book, battered and worn with age,
A record of life's long journey, memories on every page.

There were scenes of joy and sorrow, some sunshine and some rain,
Pictures of love and laughter, pictures of tears and pain,
And on each of the tattered pages was a picture of a cross,
She said, 'That's where our Saviour suffered, and died to redeem
         the lost.'

And then the dream was over and I woke to face the day,
But I'll never forget that lady as I travel along my way.
She had a quiet confidence, a hope that would never die,
In faith she had walked life's highway towards her home on high.

I met her briefly in Dreamland where fact and fiction entwine,
But the peace and calm of her gentle soul reached out and entered mine,
And I pray that God will grant me the strength to walk in His ways,
Till I meet with that lady in Heaven, at the end of my earthly days.

Jenny Porteous

HEART IN THE SKY

In the café, you play the guitar.
Dreaming notes, drifting far.
Floating high,
To the sky.
Silence. Then all applaud.
Deflated, shoulders hunched, and bored.
You cannot bear to part,
With the heart,
You left high, up in the sky.

U Johnson

TEENAGERS! WHO'D HAVE THEM?
(Dedicated to teenagers everywhere, and especially to Annie!)

Teenagers! Who'd have them?
That's what I say,
How could that sweet baby,
Have turned out this way?

Stroppy, and moody,
Hormones running riot,
Music blaring out,
Though you've yelled out - 'Be quiet!'

But, up goes the volume
And slam goes her door,
So you storm up the stairs
Just can't take any more!

The sign on her door warns . . .
Private! Enter only if you dare!
But you open it anyway,
To be met by a glare!

You turn down the volume,
Tell her that her room's a disgrace -
But that cheeky young madam
Just laughs in your face!

She turns the stereo full blast,
'I hate you' she sneers.
Where is that sweet child
That gave love all those years?

Then she flops onto her bed
And turns her face to the wall.
Teenagers! Who'd have them?
Don't understand them at all!

Oh where is that sweet babe
I bounced on my knee
Surely this *rebel*
It just cannot be!

Gone are the Barbie dolls, the tea sets and toys
Replaced by thick make-up, loud music and *boys!*
Gone are the ringlets, the ribbons and laces
All I see now are her scowls and fixed braces!

A fifteen year old with a mind of her own
No longer a baby - but not yet fully grown!
At odds with each other - just cannot agree.
But . . . if I look closely,
        In her,
            I see,
                Me!

Sylvia E L Reynolds

WHAT'S IN A NAME?

Little Jean Gurney embarked on a journey
In search of her family tree,
Well aware her surname had achieved local fame
'Twixt Norwich and Wells-next-the-sea.

Weak on genealogy but strong on astrology,
Jean read works by one 'Nostradamus',
Who'd made it quite plain that folk with her name
Would all become soldiers or farmers.

She toured areas eastern like Hoveton and Beeston
And scanned parish files at Corpusty
With the finest toothcomb. By the time she got home,
Her mood was frustrated and crusty.

She pursued her research and consulted the church
In her quest to establish a link.
She strove might and main, but all was in vain,
It practically drove her to drink!

Then a young guy named Hugh promised Jean he'd be true,
And bought her a swish wedding gown.
With minimal grief and a sigh of relief
She became, simply . . . Mrs Jean Brown.

Alan Titley

FIRST DAY

My first day at school was not good for my health
With a shirt full of starch it stood up by itself,
I was forced to wear trousers barely down to my knees
With hanky filled pockets in case of a sneeze.
I hung onto Mummy, like a limpet I clasped
And at the school gate I cried and I gasped,
But all my excuses fell alas on deaf ears
Sudden aches and bad pains, even crocodile tears.
It was then that I realised my fate indeed plight
When Mum said, 'Goodbye,' left and vanished from sight,
Then a teacher insisted we all went inside
I searched to escape but found no place to hide.
But then I saw friends and by the end of that day
We all had such fun that I wanted to stay,
So when Mummy arrived, I was filled with such sorrow
But I soon wore a smile when told, 'More school tomorrow.'

Maria Colvin

CHANNEL-HOPPING

I love to go Channel-hopping on ferry or hovercraft.
Driving down to Dover, making an early start.
Hoping to pick up a bargain before rolling off the other end.
Arriving later in Calais, or the dock in bustling Ostend.
The people are so friendly, helpful in every way.
Such wonderful architecture, oh I wish I had longer to stay!
Pastries and cakes are delicious, the coffee too is great.
I'll try and get in some shopping before it is too late.
My bags are bulging now, for me there is no stopping.
If you want something exciting to do, just try Channel-hopping.

Hazell Dennison

REQUIEM FOR AN EXILE

So you're gone at last, my friend. But how
      did you go I wonder - did you wake
        for a little and remember me?
Or did you die an old man's death
      mumbling and forgetful
          grateful
   for the night-nurse's stiff rustle
pausing by green-shaded lamps at the end of the ward?
            Or did you die hard
      like one beaten to death in the bull-ring
      asking no mercy and receiving none?
              I mourn
      for you and all the others.
Telling their tales by the alien gas-fire
or round the corner table in the coffee bar
      they haunt the empty streets at dusk
      like the evening when we said goodbye
      for the last time without knowing it
standing at the bus stop under the bitter rain.

If my tears can reach you and warm you a little
      take them, wherever you are
and the worn coin of memory for your journey.

Vanda Cutler

ENDGAME

White pawn,
Red king
Parted
By armies,
But ahead, a square lies empty.

White pawn
Moves forward
Towards the king
To stand equal for a moment at his side.

Across the squares
Across the world
Does he not see?
Does he not know - will he give answer?

Red queen
Moves forward
Guards the king
White pawn falls back, defeated and alone.

Endgame over,
Pieces swept aside
Inanimate.
The game is on again - white pawn, red king . . .

June Oliver

MY LADY FAIR

I long to see the countryside,
I long for the sweet scented air,
To kiss again those tempting lips
Of my lady so young and fair.

I want to feel the grass beneath my feet,
To sit beside a quiet stream,
Hold my lady in my arms
And in the peace I will dream.

There came a day she laughed at me,
And my lady ran away to hide,
She said she loved another
And long into the night I cried.

They found us together next morning,
Blood stained her pretty hair.
They took her lovely body from me,
My lady so young and fair.

Now I am in a place, so dark and tall.
Someone is always there,
So I shall never again be alone
With my lady so young and fair.

Ruby Havelin

SPRING

Fluffy, yellow chicks, sleeping in the nest,
Easter Bunny comes to stay, he's our springtime guest.
Daffodils die, and tulips come up,
Little springtime babies, include kittens and pups.

Tiny, white lambs stand on wobbly legs,
At last mums hang the washing out with bright yellow pegs.
Daffodils and crocuses pop up all around,
Stray chickens making nests are always to be found.

We take springtime for granted,
As summer flowers can be planted.
So listen to the blue tits going 'Sing, sing, sing,'
And be happy, happy, happy, 'cos it's
Spring, spring, spring!

Jessica Handley (9)

UNTITLED

I am alone in the low cave of night,
The waves sing gently on the pebbled shore,
The world, secretive in its weird delight,
Shadows and weaves and darkens more and more.

Possessed by wind and wave and blinded space,
And the wild power that breaks upon the weak
When night has gathered up their self disgrace,
And thinking stands to let emotion speak.

I would die now, and take this living fire
To bridge mortality, not death come yawning
Hand to the mouth of a half dead desire,
When I am old, in the low ebb of the morning.

Mary Colquhoun

LOVE ON THE NO 66

His hair was a work of art,
A coronet of golden-tipped spikes that
saluted another day;
And hers - a wild curling mass, that desperately
fought the harnessing of a myriad of ribbons.

It was just a sidelong glance,
But he caught it, through the sheet of breath-warmed
glass that smelled of smoke and towns,
And spinning, tried to trap the look full on -
but only met the solemnity of a dozen pairs of eyes.

Crimson-faced he picked his way
through the limb-spiked aisle, until the stark void
of pavement held him steady.
Then daylight. Thin air to vanish into -
Can one really vanish? The unyielding buildings gave no clues.

The girl with the hair had gone.
But she was filling his mind and his heart with
a sickening pleasure.
He would find her if it took forever;
And a dozen pairs of eyes closed with suburban tedium.

Jean Skinner

Autumn Again

Already
Leaves are coming down
And I am not ready.

Not ready for summer to end,
Switched off suddenly.

Not ready for cooler mornings,
Terrace no longer warm.

Not ready to wear my kimono,
Too cool for nakedness outdoors.

Not ready to think about wood,
Keeping the log basket full.

Not ready for my own autumn,
Creaking body slowing down.

Not ready to move on,
Beginning to consider old age.

Not ready for that,
Not ready for anything like that.

Not remotely ready.

First
The falling leaves of autumn,
Then the winter.

Richard Maslen

POEM/SONG

Is the love worth the pain,
endless struggles, endless strain?
Three days of it being bliss,
then four days of an ocean of tears,
Yet an amazing feeling from his kiss,
followed by turmoil and all my fears,
Only he's responsible for my smile deep within,
wanting a loving family life to begin,
Yet being the strength for everyone,
knowing the battle has only just started,
to stick by this man: it's far from won,
two innocent children to really love,
Showing them fun, protection, trying to rise above,
Believing I'd never feel this love again,
the attraction simply wouldn't be the same,
Having faith but can't do what I should do,
wanting to support him and work it through.
How do you know when to call it a day?
How do you push such a strong love away?
Strength coming from I don't know where,
What are you doing? people say to me,
But such a true sense of I really do care,
Why won't he open his eyes and see?
Why won't he open his eyes and see?

Nina Bates

TEMPUS FUGIT

A thousand years,
Ten thousand or a million,
Will humanity be gone,
And nothing remain,
But ruins crumbled by wind
And washed by rain.
Why have monuments
That none will see,
Or records none will read?
Or is each moment
Fixed in its own place,
With its own significance,
Its own eternal face?
Are past and present to be
Ingredients of time's complexity?

Vera Boyle

BURNT MILL

Working at the window of the mill
The noise of falling water soothes
The labour of the day, the mind fills
With visions of long ages past, smoothes
The unsteady hands of new apprentices.

Here the heron with his searching bill
Parades the silent pond for food.
Wagtails flit and bob below the rill
As the inward eye begins to brood
On happiness in large parentheses.

The wheel turns no more, yet the mill stream
Flows. A purple mist enshrouds the lane
Faint hoof beats sound and draw into my dream
Creaking carts piled high with sacks of grain
Centuries spin by as in a trance.

As the senses fade into the past
The fragrance of old leather lingers
In the dusty air as if held fast
With knowing art and skilful fingers.
Famine, plague, black death and fire advance.

Now here in the corner Caxton tends
His press, and the age of books begins
And so here where the winding lane ends
The living word uncovers all our sins.
And the world is now as it was then.

Technology advances and books retreat
There is sadness here in the shadows
Yet no thought of admitting defeat
Kingfishers skim and dive in the shallows
So near, so far, from the noise of men.

John Stanbridge

KILLER

I hide in the shadows
Of this time last year.
Day and night mingled
In the depths of despair.

I hardly dare face
The bad times we had.
It makes me so tearful
And oh so very sad,

You couldn't get yourself up
Or back in to bed.
Cried out for help
And struggled for breath.

The cancer was eating
Away at your flesh.
Your kidneys were failing
Your brain was distressed.

You didn't want food
And wouldn't take drink.
Should I force down your tablets
Or leave you to sink

Desperately in to your last and longest sleep.

Jane Jones

THIS LAND

What happened to this land they knew,
The grass so green and filled with dew,
The land for which they gave their lives,
The land that made widows of their wives,
For they went to fight to save this land
The man the boy with gun in hand,
They went and fought those terrible years,
They went and fought through all their fears,
And for all of those who failed to return
There was a message, but we didn't learn,
What's gained from war, but death and pain
Death and destruction, it's so insane,
But they saved this land, the man and boy
But if they saw it now there would be no joy,
For what we've done to this land of ours,
The tarmac jungle, concrete, the scars,
If they came back now, after all these years
On the grass there would be, not dew, but tears.

Peter Jessop

AUSCHWITZ

Inside the rooms, it is dark, damp,
Ceaseless scent of death is deep.
Victims starved, cursed with cramp -
Children too young, too abandoned to sleep.
Mothers frantic, unable to save their brown eyed young,
Cling to them insanely.
Until their number is up,
Snatched away grimly, ungainly.

Inside the rooms it is unsilent,
Unceremonious deaths fitfully heard,
As the men, unmoved - violent
Perform some horrific vivisection even more absurd
than the last.
Children panic, want to feel safe - hear ghastly sounds,
Confused, chaotic monstrosities within the tomb,
Where each day, naked thousands are found
Suffocated in some cold, stark, ungodly room.

Inside the rooms, the dark haired puppets scream
At the manic shadows on the floor,
Stench of singed, charred flesh stabs the air,
Piercing each Semite to the core.
The Elders drop, mutter hopeless prayers,
Hearts crippled by collapse of corpses where they fall.
Dead eyes, turgid as a hung man's stare,
Stillness breaks as massacred innocents call.

D Hayward

THE CONTRARINESS OF NATURE

What awesome power, what beauty, what joy nature can bring
Newborn life, awakenings, the promises of spring
Gentle sea breezes lapping a sun kissed shore
Changing mood, mighty winds blow, mountainous waves roar

Magnificence of nature's wildernesses, forests, continents of icy terrain
Fearsome thunderstorm, typhoon, tornado, hurricane
Volcanoes erupting, earthquakes shaking and convulsing
Natural disasters, destruction, death and world's landscapes changing

Noble nature controlling seasons, tides and weather
All creatures great and small, giant trees and purple heather
Warm spring sunshine, gentle showers of rain
Continual reawakenings making everything new again

The infinity and wonder of outer space
Spinning the universe at incredible pace
Whatever nature's moods and plans may be
Adverse forces, disasters mastered by man's ingenuity

K G Johnson

CONTEMPLATION

Stiff limbs, slow moving
Weary, lost
The will to try whate'er the cost.
Determination on a face filled with pain!
A smile in place.
Some surrender, what's the use.
We'll sit around,
We'll call a truce.
Bygone days, dreams so real
Are all we have, and we can feel
The pleasures of an age now past.
We'll sleep and savour
Rest at last!

Winifred Knell

IMAGES

When in your youth, when dark and cold,
did the images unfold
of night-time demons, ghosts and fright,
and did they scare you through the night?

Did you hide beneath the sheet
afraid to look, afraid to peep
into the dark, into the black,
afraid of that, which may look back?

A flickering light, a hazy sound
and you felt sure they were around.
Remembering what someone had said,
or did they lurk beneath your bed?

You dare not look, for if you did
you'd soon find out, where they now hid.
You lay there, cowering through the night
awaiting dawn's most welcome light.

And when it came, relief came too,
you then felt brave, knew what to do.
You weren't afraid when it was light
but then, you'd face another night.

Where in the shadows they would hide
and slowly creep to your bedside
to taunt you as you go to sleep
but you're too scared to have a peep.

Now that I'm old, or so they say,
and had a dream the other day.
When in a sweat I woke and found
I was alone, no ghosts around.

None did lurk, beneath my bed,
nor in dark corners for now instead
I need not look, and know I'll find,
that they live only, in my mind.

Richard Lee Nettleton

MIDGE

She dashes to the Beetle, my frenzied, manic Midge,
Excited at the prospect: our journey's end Rodbridge . . .
The driver's window open - her ears fly in the wind.
A passing truck comes very close,
Missing her whiskers, just missing her nose -
My crazy, manic friend!

We finally reach the prairie (nose and whiskers still intact!)
I open the car door half-an-inch and she springs out just like that!

I'll catch her up around the bend - she's nowhere to be seen . . .
And then I see her twinkling eyes - like a hunting lioness there she lies,
The long, lush grass is no disguise, for this local safari queen.

I walk, she runs; I throw, she fetches; the routine's understood,
But respectfully we quieten down on entering the wood.
I feed the robins with bread and nuts
Whilst she, like a tigress, licks make-believe cuts,
And occasionally pinches their food!

Our safari is over; we return to the car.
Her legs caked in blood - but of course it's just mud . . .
One can't take this story too far!

She travels home breathless from chasing her prey -
The stalking and hunting a frightening display!
Rabbits and squirrels, and sometimes a frog,
Escape certain death from this menacing dog!
But she allows them to live one more day . . .

She springs from the car and waits by her gate.
The tigress returns in a mud-splattered state.
A quick towelling down and a pat on the head,
Water - food - and a cosy, warm bed.
I'll see her tomorrow - on that I depend -
My frantic, frenzied, menacing friend.

Jennie Pudney

THE SPARROW

His shabby coat with colours scant portrays
This poor communicant, in nature's church of
Open sky where all God's little creatures fly.
But not for him this priestly white of doves
High up in flight who dive and turn so acute
And dip their wing tips in salute.

He doesn't crave the robin's redbreast nor
The place does he aspire among the other birds
With plumage grand that visits our shores
From some foreign lands, but for his part this
Little chap likes nothing better than a scrap.
But all through his life his bread and butter
Then has another punch up in the gutter.
His peers with a great intellect often die from
Sheer neglect.

On frozen pond, branch or fence as they all
Seem to lack good common-sense,
When winter winds chill you to the marrow well
You'll seldom see the little sparrow as he
Hides himself away from view in nature's church
Beneath a pew. He is no dunce this little bird
But be assured he is one of Mother Nature's
Great survivors . . .

Poacher Prince

SNOWFALL

Cyprus trees in early March
Bow down with weight of heavy snow
Fierce blizzard in the afternoon
Blanketing the muddy fields.

Rooftops sprinkled powder like
With a dusting - wintry scene
Nightly comes the dangerous frost
Icy are the country lanes.

This is but an Arctic blast
Lasting short - the lengthening days
Soon sunlight will produce a thaw
As seen from seat in Norwich train.

Thus frozen are the Norfolk wastes
Near houses new in ancient Diss
Spring with warmth is close at hand
A change of climate coming soon.

Steve Glason

LETTING GO

(For my children Louise, Samia, Phaedra and Jamal)

There comes a time when we have to let go of
Our mother's apron strings and start life on our own,
But no one said it would be easy.
But it was easy compared to what was to come,
Because now I've got to do what my mother did . . .

How do you let go after so many years
Of long sleepless nights when you end up in tears
Of wiping red noses and bathing grazed knees
Of handing out money with no guarantees
Of receiving as much as a 'Thanks Mum you're great'
But you do it regardless, and when they are late
You can't go to sleep till you hear them come in
No matter what age it's always the same.
But at last comes the time when the youngest leaves home

Now it's Radio 2 and the lock's off the phone
So why do I feel like someone has died
I walk round the house feeling empty inside
The rooms all look tidy, the posters no more,
Just a faint trace of Blu-tac on the back of a door.
Towels all hang neatly in a bathroom so clean
With sparkling taps and mirrors that gleam.
So why do I wish for clothes on the floor
For ear splitting music and worries galore,
And why, when I'm finally here on my own,
Do I wish they were here with me, living at home.

Jeanne Sinclair

REARRANGING

My box-room doesn't have too much space for my memories,
So I wear them behind a ploy of bland expressions and pleasantries.
I look up behind a barricade of shower gel
And condensation; as muddled voices are played over the radio.
I await for inspiration or a cheque to arrive
To keep the wheels turning however slowly they move
In the winter months of stark reality.

Laurence De Calvert

A COUNTRY LANE

The warm summer evening breeze,
Sped through the country lane
Moving the branches, and rustling the leaves.

Two lovers strolling along its path
Had their cheeks caressed by its movements
As it hurried along past

The warmth and the movement
Evoked emotional sighs

As they looked across
Into each other's eyes

The messages sent were the same to each other,
Throughout all ages, of sweethearts and lovers

The breeze carried, through on to mown fields of hay
Paused as it espied two more as they lay

They too were enthralled
By love's story of old

But the breeze carried on
Till its warmth turned to cold

Ron Robson

SPRING COMES AGAIN

The sky is blue,
and there's snow on the ground,
a few cotton wool clouds,
just drifting around.

Now amongst all this,
just peeping through
are snowdrops and violets
and primroses too.

The bulbs are all pointing,
up towards the sky,
the sun is shining through,
and the birds are flying high.

The birds are busy,
as spring is near.
With nests to build,
and food to share.

There'll be buzzing of bees,
and buds on the trees,
awaiting the spring
and beautiful green leaves -

- to shelter the birds,
from the wind and the rain,
winter has gone,
and spring comes again.

M Williams

A Day In The Nursery

We come at nine, our spirits high,
Hats and coats, off they fly.
The boys and girls start to play
'Til all at once they're heard to say
'The toilet please to spend a penny;
So through we trail - oh, so many.
Milk and biscuits eat with pleasure
Sweets and bananas without measure
Out to play, don hats and coats,
Shoes and scarves, caps and boots.
Sand tray full, sand tray emptying -
Not to waste it, oh - so tempting.
In to lunch, wash those hands
Sit at table, great demands.
Now say grace, then sweep the floor,
Lost your chance to ask for more.
Settle down to television, then heave sigh for peace and quiet
And make the most of those few minutes
'Cause any time there'll be a riot.
Plasticine and pastry, painting - take your pick
Make a gorgeous mess - clear it up - right quick
Half past two, what a blessing,
Time to dress, no more messing.
Sweep and tidy, turn off stoves.
Pile the chairs, no more moves.
Smile at parents, say 'Yes they're good'
Tongue in cheek then hit the road.

Winifred Forster

TRANSFORMING LIGHT

Transforming light within our mind,
Reaching miles afar;
Across the void of space and time,
Returning rays of wonder are.

Translucent light we're passing by;
For a journey never-ending.
Revolving in an orbit finding,
Returning back from whence we came.
Precision in our timely home,
All life remains the same.

Created from a simple pattern
Found through searching fashion;
Of the never-ending plain
Within our souls we find
That we are all the same.

Continuing of our journey;
Through all time and space
A man made rule to guide us;
And keep order in this place.

Christi Annie

WORDS' WORTH

How inadequate our words can be.
Between the mouth that speaks them
And the ears that hear
There sometimes seems a barrier -
Sometimes a chasm -
Sometimes a howling tumult.

Subtle shades of meaning
Are lost on some
Or never found.

Sincerity despised
And honesty repelled
Make nonsense of it all.

Did Shakespeare talk?
Did Shakespeare have a ready wit
In mundane conversation?
Could he feel sympathy
For those who searched for words
Without success?

Were some great writers
So appalled by what they heard
They wrote to make amends
For desecration wrought
By those content with
Verbal sludge.

Verbal alchemy
Must be the quest.
The words are there;
It is how we used them
That will lead us
To the gold.

Hugh Mullarkey

TEN THOUSAND YEARS AND THREE FEET OF CABLE

I'm only one emotion
and a pointless evolutionary leap
away from an all winter hibernation
complexity a technological advance
speeding up time to what effect
this is quicker that is quicker
if I breathe any quicker
I'll suffocate my senses

simple pleasures for a simple mind
let me tone down my nakedness
so that which I own
will never upset
instead push me further
out to sea
on a wave of incompleteness

Darren Powles

REVENANT

In the silent dark a pheasant
starts up, flying,
raking the pitch of night with harsh
primeval crying.
An icy breeze is fingering through
the bare-boned trees,
up and down the frozen furrows
to the distant seas.

A figure sometimes rises then,
in secret hours to roam
along the ancient pathways,
follows the north wind home.

On the cliff there is a shadow
falling, steeling
over the grassy slopes, cast by
a strange light reeling
from a tower to the horizon,
across the silvered waves
that cover the former land
and long sunken graves.

The lost soul claims a birthright there,
glides up in waking dreams
along black lonely tackways,
drawn by the golden beams.

Andria Cooke

GIFTS

As I look around me
Inside this tiny flat
There are lots of treasures
Bits and pieces, this and that

Things I have kept for a long time
Do not amount to much
But every week I go around
I dust, and lovingly touch

There are photographs of family
Little smiles of joy
Granddaughters and my grandson
'Grandma's lovely boy'

Memories of yesteryear
Pictures of a black cat
She has been gone - a year
Was it really as long as that?

Then there are my plants
I feed and water well
Living pieces of greenery
They give me a feeling - no smell

A feeling of a future
For they are living things
Needing care and attention
The pleasures that they bring

These hands of mine are stiff
But Lord if you are able
Please help me care for my gifts
Keep me in charge of my table

Jenny Campling

The Vacuum Of Death!

You remain forever young until
　　　　　you die old.
From whence you mysteriously enter
　　　　　another world so bold;
Where time doesn't exist for, to be sold
And to caress, isn't necessarily to hold;
For you're now,
　　　　living with the heavenly fold.

A place, so much different to earth
　　　for there is no pain of birth;
Although your freedom
　　　　remains your wisdom
And your wisdom explains your freedom
　　　　　for what it is worth!

Dave White

PASTIMES

Now I've retired
What shall I do?
I'll have much more time now
Than I ever used to

I could become a gardener
They tell me it's good
For my health
Or I could make a 'cock up'
Of 'do it yourself'

I could travel afar
To see what I've missed
Or I could take up drinking
And spend the time p***ed

I could read a lot
Or watch the box
Or take up horse riding
And chasing the fox

I could go sky diving
And hang the expense
But I'd probably end up
Skewered on someone's picket fence

I thought I'd try donating sperm
So went there on the bus
After they finished laughing
They said 'We'll call you
Don't call us'

I could try to help people
My time is for free
But the Samaritans would probably
End up with them ringing me

I could try bungee jumping
That sounds a winner
But on the rebound I'd
Probably throw up my dinner

I could try water sports
Above or below it
But I think I'll take thing easy
And just become a poet

James Valentine Sullivan

THE LAST GOODBYE

She lies quiet, still in the hospital bed,
No more pounding of the heart,
Sightless eyes closed in rest, no more breathing.
The whirling fan has had its say,
The song it sang was the same each day.
And while it sang it shakes its head.
Is there no hope to the mystery of living?

Early evening light filters through slatted windows,
The sky is gathering again
Building pressure in the silent room
To mingle with the sorrow and pain
And her love which is there to see.
She leaves behind a cherished memory
Of godliness, fairness and honesty.

A quiet tap on the door signals us to go.
My son and I kiss her warm face,
Our steps to the door are measured and slow,
Leaving a lady we cannot replace.
She has her faith, she needs no proof
Of facing her Maker to find the truth.

We make the ground floor without a word
A heart that is broken will be hard to mend.
We pass the lounge, the tinkle of tea cups are heard.
Many sit and wait, appointments to attend.
On the exit doors that open wide
Arms outstretched to welcome us outside.
We draw in breath and drink the air.
The sun begins to sink, the clouds a billowy pink,
Trees sway and the birds nest in fear
While the leaves mourn and shed a tear.

E S Peaford

A LOST SOUL

I held you close and stroked your cheek,
But still you didn't wake.
You looked so perfect lying there,
But no sound did you make.

I'd longed for your arrival,
Looked forward to the day.
I've never known the reason why
God took you away.

Did he need another angel?
Was there work He wanted done?
I only know that on that day
He took away my son.

We didn't share a moment,
A breath you didn't take,
I held you for the last time
As my heart began to break.

Every time I look upon
A mother and her son
I feel the pain of knowing
That your life had not begun.

This pain still lives within me,
Each second, every day,
And the emptiness within my heart
Will never go away.

I'd give anything to have you back,
To watch you grow and play,
And to know the special person
That you would have been today.

Alice Ackland

THE WHITE SPRAY HORSE

Glide the silk sands of the sea
Never to be sold
The beauty, jewels, crystal, ice
Pearl white spray the waves to hold.

They stare, they dance
To the steady applause
As the ripples of waves sing,
But still it does roam the ocean moors.

The dawn does fall
The search continues on -
On a sea of shimmering gold
Like a sandy dream gone wrong.

But the fiery life never ceases
Through the ocean course
Blue, emerald, red yet gold
The life of the white spray horse.

Hannah Webb (13)

WAITING PATIENTLY

Early or late it doesn't matter when
I have to cross this busy road, heck I could of then.
I have to be extra careful in the fog.
Don't want to end up like that poor hedgehog.

You can be ages just waiting here.
Cars and lorries buzzing around everywhere.
I wonder if anyone will slow down and flash.
Then across this busy road I could dash.

What am I thinking while I'm waiting.
Just that there's mad people overtaking.
Everyone always seems in such a hurry.
They don't want to be late they always worry.

Hooray what's this I see.
Yes someone has actually noticed me.
As he flashes his lights I run across the road fast.
A quick sigh of relief I'm over the other side at last.

I have to cross this road to get to my job.
Things we do to earn a few bob.
Plus I know I'm helping someone out.
To me that's what it's all about.

And I have to do this when I leave off again.
It's okay as long as it's not pouring with rain.
But it's lovely to be out and about on my bike.
The fresh air and lovely countryside is what I like.

Kathy Buckley

SUNRISE OVER THE CHILTERNS

All men may see their sunrise
     Around our world today -
None could be more beautiful
     Than the Chiltern hills display
Bright vermilion, dazzling gold
     Slow changes every minute
Fantastic colours now unfold
     With glaring pictures in it!

Pink fleecy clouds drifting above
     Edged with purest gold
As if mountain ranges on and on -
     The peeks stand out so bold!
Pastel blue of skies beyond
     Now a changing into green
I gaze amazed, no artist's brush -
     Could 'ere record that scene

Painted for me, mere man!
     Oh! Lord why do I fail?
To sing Thy praises constantly
     Reach out beyond man's veil -
See above, but emptiness
     When your promises are such -
That eye of man can never see
     The total beauty of Thy touch!

Geoffrey S S Wilyman

THE CURSE OF MALEFICE

She hears a footstep on the stair,
But whose? Of this she is unaware.
She does not know that it is I,
And yet she sweats as the seconds pass by.
Oh, farmer's daughter, your time is now,
You will never milk another cow.
For your father has been evil towards me,
And that my friend can never be.

Your 'dear daddy' hired me,
To set his loved one's spirit free.
How was I supposed to heal
An illness progressing like a wheel?
The farmer called me a 'crooked spey-wife',
And so for this I must take your life.
Every girl in your family,
Will feel all my misery.

The arrogant farmer seemed to think
That this will end as quick as a blink.
How stupid could your father be?
I don't think that he really knows me.
This curse that I am laying here,
Will never, ever end my dear.
In the morning he will start to fret,
Your death will shock him tomorrow, pet!

Sarah Evans-Wrench

THE REMARKABLE MRS SMITH

The remarkable Mrs Smith
lives next-door to me
on a sunny day
she hangs her washing
out to air and dry.

She talks over the garden fence
showing interest in the town,
the country, the world and me,
in my meagre existence.

The remarkable Mrs Smith
doesn't have a Mr Smith
lives with her boy and girl,
lovely children,
who play ball in the garden.

She invites me for coffee
on dank, rainy days
and I sit happily
in her kitchen, among
the sweet smelling herbs.

The remarkable Mrs Smith
full of life and laughter
lifts my spirit, every time
she looks at me,
the dowdy old woman,
that I am.

Marion Roberts

EAST ANGLIAN CHURCHES

Old churches stand
Where'er the eye can see.
East Anglian churches -
Steeped in history.
Some towers round -
But mostly towers square.
Thousands of families
Must have worshipped there.

Stained-glass windows
Telling of stories true.
Crumbling tombstones
Belonging to people who
Once lived and loved
In ancient days of yore,
Their records etched
On marble by the door.

And still they stand
For all to view around -
East Anglian churches
Admired, as they surround.

Pam Dutton

STORY OF A SAINT

He was always gentle, ever true
and has the best stone in the graveyard,
did all the shopping though thanks never knew,
still has the best stone in the graveyard.

Pulled out her chair, did all her to ease,
and he has the best stone in the graveyard,
helped all he could though he never could please,
but he has the best stone in the graveyard.

Loved her so dear knowing no love returned,
but given the best stone in the graveyard,
gave all his money yet his love she spurned,
though she gave him the best stone in the graveyard.

Lived for her only with no thought of gain,
but she bought the best stone in the graveyard,
gave his life in the end to spare her pain,
so deserved the best stone in the graveyard.

Maybe she loved him but just didn't know it,
though she bought the best stone in the graveyard,
maybe she loved him but just couldn't show it,
till she bought the best stone in the graveyard.

Madge H Paul

SHEPHERD

The sheep are restless and fidgety this morning -
scrabbling to see what treats are in store.
What tricks will he get them to perform today?
Will he tease them with games they all find such a bore?
Watch the tears welling up in the eyes of the lost ones
who scratch feebly on the page to find meaning in puzzles
he torments them with, every endless lesson.

He cries out, and they stumble and dodge his sharp stare,
looking innocent, unarmed, not daring to think
for themselves. What's the answer? hands reaching for the ceiling,
hoping God will provide, and care for their feelings,
while the teacher, bloodless, enforces each rule
and the sheep dare not bleat, struck dumb by this school.

Howard Young

A KEY TO LIVING

Life was given us for living
to love, laugh and play,
It seems in boxes we are placed
but did not come that way.

Life we are told is precious
free or so they say,
then why the chains restricting flight
shackled more each day.

We walk along life's path but once
to enjoy as best we can,
not to gaze from buildings tall
built by other man.

Life was meant for living
not just to tow the line,
if things were not the way they are
would not life be fine?

Let's take these faceless people
we should really make them pay,
lock them in a great big box
and throw the key away.

Audrey Williams

THE BUTTERFLY

'Neath a shady tree my love
Doth lie on sun warmed hay,
Whist gentle breezes softly cool
This beauteous summer's day.

I alone thus with my love
Should happiest mortal be,
But hath some way offended her,
She speaketh not to me.

A glimpse of colour now I see
From out the azure sky,
And there to settle on her breast
A lovely butterfly.

Charmed is she by his caress
And sends him not away,
With open wings he makes his rest,
Close to her heart now lay.

My love doth smile to see him so
Spares not a glance for me,
Oh butterfly, sweet butterfly,
I would that I were thee.

P W Pidgeon

AVELEY

Aveley, where do I start,
back in the days of horse and cart.
No not then I wasn't alive,
How about the year 1995.

The little village is small and clean,
Some people around are really mean.
Above all that there is somewhere,
When I am bored I like to go there.

A great stretch of football pitches,
At the back of the field there is a few
shallow ditches.

Football goals with nets tied tight,
I tell you it's footballers' delight.

Adam Deas (12)

UNREQUITED LOVE

I awoke this morning
And felt so very sad
The boy, my daughter loved so much
Has shattered the dreams she had.

He left her for another girl
With hair so curly bright
As pretty as a picture
With eyes like stars on a dark, dark night.

I'm sure this romance will never last
This girl is fickle with the boys
Once she's won them over
She treats them like discarded toys.

It's very hard as a mother
To see your child in pain
I want to take the hurt away
And make her whole again

My daughter's heart will heal in time
Of that there is no doubt
She will find someone else to love
More worthy and devout.

Time is passing oh so fast
My daughter is happy again
She still has all her life ahead
After all she is only ten.

Sylvia Hall

RIDING ON THE WIND

If ever at a loss
Trying to be boss
Being at an angle
Stuck in a triangle
Hit from pillar to post
Feeling as a ghost
In our happy throng
Yet everything goes wrong
Keeping one's end together
Forever and ever
Things to be found
We go round and round
There is a shout
Everything is thrown out
Some are at fought
It comes to nought
Although it's not fare
Sent here and there
Walking with hand in glove
It's just a son's love

Anthony Higgins

ANGEL OF MINE

As I sit on the cliff top
And gaze out to sea
An angel from heaven
Is sitting with me
With wings soft as silk
And a voice sweet 'n' low
Wiping my tears -
As gently they flow
I feel that I know him
Something is there . . .
There's a look in his eyes
That I've seen in a stare
My heart though it's broken
Is somehow at ease
As I sense him beside me
Or is it the breeze?
There on the cliff top
As the sun sets on the sea
You will find me so peaceful
With my angel with me . . .

Lisa Bristow

MY BIRTHDAY PARTY

My birthday is 21st of March
But I had the party on 17th March
All my friends and family come to join in the fun
And gave me all nice presents
And I ate nice food that went in my tum
And I had a drink. It was Coke and rum.

Emma Perfect

A BROTHER'S GRIEF

This mind that sees the cloudy sky,
These memories, that provoke a million tears,
Of family loss and brotherly ties,
This evil, in charity, that pumps the tears.

Gnawing like thunder, across a cloudy plain,
These tears gush out, like a bitter rain,
Soaking one's cheeks, like an inward soul,
Achieving as little, as an unscored goal.

These memories deny the years that have passed,
As misery surmounts the glowing feast,
Plunging one's spirits, to a childhood past,
As the tide of life ebbs, for this mortal's release.

These cheeks, anointed by a myriad tears,
These brothers, whose laughter defied a thousand fears,
This soul, tormented by this heavenly deal,
This love, this death, this grief, that only time can heal.

Dennis Scott

THE 'SAVIOUR' OF NOTTING HILL

*(Special constable, confidant, John R H Christie, executed
July 15th 1953 for the murder of seven women)*

She was a village girl with country ways
Who'd tired of swilling pigs and milking cows:
'I must move out if I want better days,
The city lights are prettier than ploughs;
These curtain-twitching windows get me down -
Your every move is chronicled round here,
I'm heading for your wonders trendy town
Where I can 'let my hair down' without fear.'
She met him in a cosy dim-lit bar -
A homely friendly man with gentle ways;
This lonely girl thought him a guiding star,
In her new life it was a pleasant phase.
What freedom! With no idle village chat
For walking with her 'saviour' to his flat.

A Yorkshire lad, he'd come south years ago,
Now middle-aged and prim, he posed no threat.
The lonely and the lost - the way he'd show,
And many were so grateful that they'd met
To tell their troubles to this caring man,
In pubs and cafes out of the fog and grime.
They had no inkling of his monstrous plan,
To them he was so wise and had the time.
Yes! He'd the time to make up for the past:
His tyrant Father and that mocking girl;
Those painful memories - away he'd cast -
The repressed 'flag of manhood' he'd unfurl
To raise on high, free from shame and fear.
But for the sacrificed, there was no bier.

Peter Haines

MY MOTHER TONGUE

They smile at me kindly
And replenish my tea cup.
The talk washes around me,
I have trouble keeping up.
Your arm I once could lean on,
And you helped me to be strong.
But now I'm like an alien
Who's lost her mother tongue

They laugh and pass around the cakes
And catch each other's eye;
I sit quite still to evade the ache,
And struggle not to cry.
With you I was much stronger
When you offered me your hand.
Now I feel like a foreigner
In some quite alien land

Everyone's so kind to me
I need not be alone.
They ask me round to lunch or tea,
They write to me and phone.
But all I really want is you,
And when the sun goes down,
To be no more a foreigner
Who's lost her mother tongue.

Polly Clarke

THE IMPACT OF MOTOR NEURONE DISEASE

I was like you,
I had a job too.
I attended meetings
and coped with various greetings.
I responded appropriately,
and spoke beautifully.
I kept up to date,
attending many a school fête.
I dined in restaurant or wine bar,
driving there in my car.
When enjoying a concert song,
I could be seen dancing and singing along.
Organising children and their care,
was tended to and always fair.
I could run for a train,
and moan about things being a 'pain'.
I could join in conversation,
being capable of normal participation.
Maintaining interest in world wide news,
was easy like changing a fuse.
To operate the remote control,
whilst I ate a sausage roll,
demanded no excessive exertion,
and minimal comprehension.
I wore smart clothes,
my favourite flower was a rose.
Make-up was immaculate,
whilst possessing the ability to articulate.
One day all that altered,
emotion and speech faltered.
Mobility disappeared,
Lightwriter and Hoist appeared.

Wheelchairs replaced my legs
and conversation turned to PEGS . . .
No longer in control,
I feel I've lost my soul,
I sit unable to be the 'doer'
the disease stealing more and more.
I pine for all I've lost,
independence at great cost.
No longer able to respond,
and maintain the family bond . . .
I wait for death,
dreading my last breath.
I ask you to look beyond this 'shell',
and see the story of which I tell,
'I was like you,
I had a job too . . .'

Liz Edmonds

Nobody Is Going To Ruin Me

You never said why you abused me,
You never said why you made me cry,
You never asked me what was wrong those days,
You never loved me more than you loved yourself.
Once you swore to always love me,
And always honour me, protect me,
Now you want to know who I've slept with,
Who I've dated, who I've sinned with.
You throw a fit like a woman, break my things,
I slowly poison you with silence, my means to an end.
I hope the wife you take will leave you for another girl,
I hope the family you raise will rob you blind and leave you in Hell.
I hope for you no happiness, no joy, no light,
And I curse you down to that place with no escape,
Where there are no windows, no doors,
And the only locks are on the evil deeds of your past.
What you've done to me I forgive to save my own soul,
But what you've done to me you will atone for,
We all must pay when our personal Judgement Days are cast.
This is the End, the Death, the Close, the Last.

Danielle Green

WHO

Who will look after you,
When you're sad and blue,
And who will look after you
When your skies are grey,
And who will look after you
Chasing your demons far away.
No monsters shall ever touch you
Nor fear, nor want, nor doubt,
For I shall be here for you
Casting all the bad things out.
I will be your port
Your life raft in stormy seas,
I will be your anchorage
Your place or safety from life's breeze.
I will be your haven.
No harm will come to you,
For I shall be here always
Protecting you in everything you do.
This is my pledge my promise
As God is my witness from above,
I shall do all these things willingly
As a token of my love.

Frederick M Thomas

MY FAMILY'S HAD A STROKE

I used to be a guitar player, rated fairly high,
Then when I lost my guitar hand, I thought I'd like to die,
My wife goes out to work each day,
In weather thin and thick,
She never had ambitions
To work among the sick,
Some women have vocations
To one day be a nurse,
But my wife only goes to work
To earn to fill her purse,
So looking after invalids
Was never quite her bag,
So what she has to do today
Is something of a drag.
My daughter was a featured singer
In her daddy's bands,
Until he got hit by a stroke,
That paralysed his hand.
She's getting on now with her life,
She's buying herself a flat,
She doesn't sing much these days,
My stroke's to blame for that!
So all the world's turned upside-down,
It really is no joke,
For two who were in perfect health
Now suffer from my stroke.
One who never was a nurse
Works in a nursely way,
And fills in forms like phone books,
For a meagre carer's pay.
She tends my needs by day and night,
Her labours never cease,
Hoping for the chance one day
To find some rest and peace.

Who've had this bleedin' stroke.

Mick Nash

ONE WISH

A girl sat with long golden hair
All alone on a chair,
She gave a cry of sadness
As she watched her brother complete his badness.

She had a thought of school in her mind
The boys and girls weren't very kind.
They teased her mainly about her hair
Which really was very unfair.

For this young girl never did a thing wrong
And would sit at her desk enchanted by a song.
She sat alone as she did in the flat
Wishing she could fly like a bat.

But wishes never did come true
Why? she didn't have a clue.
If only she had one wish
She wouldn't use it on a silver dish.

Instead it would make the bullies go away
She might even get friends one day
For if she did, she wouldn't be forlorn
Neither would she be alone.

Kathryn Mason (12)

THE SEED

In this grey land
that looks so bland
not much grows
but in the darkness glows
a tiny seed.
By the morning
rain is falling
to germinate this infant
as it grows
there's things it knows
and there's things it must learn

It must grow towards the light
it must shelter from the night
when the land looks dark and grey
unrolls its petals in bright array

In the darkness
there it glows
from a tiny seed
such splendour grows

And whoever sees this beauty
will know the meaning of pain
for as quickly as it grew
it will disappear again
what's left behind
you will remember
when the world looks dark
and the light surrenders
not much grows
but in the darkness glows
a tiny seed.

Sharon Birch

GRANDAD'S TEAPOT

There it do sit upon the dresser,
The teapot Gran gave to him, God bless her.
'Tom,' she said, 'this little pot's
Got magic powers, believe or not.'

'Don't be daft, you silly girl,'
He chided as her plain met purl.
O'er clicking needles, their eyes did smile.
He knew that she could he beguile.

He remembered when she was young,
How he'd loved her and the songs he'd sung.
Fifty years on, they were still in love.
But Our Lord had called her from above.

His teapot, he observed one day,
Had quite turned round the other way.
He pondered how such could be,
And what was meant for him to see.

Then there came an urgent call:
'Come, Gramps, and see this wall.'
A great, wide, crack in the old red bricks.
They'd spotted it in the time of Nick's.

Grandad's teapot now holds sway.
He's turned it right round the other way.
Greatly respected, there it do sit,
Where Grandma used to sit and knit.

John Teddy

WHAT A LIFE!

Pussy Wallah loves to wallow
Underneath the pussy-willow.

Pussy pauses in her wallow,
Puss pursues some flighty fleases.

Pussy pauses, pussy listens;
Pussy hears a little rustle.
Is it mouses? Pussy pounces,
Misses mouses, snuffles, sneezes.

Pussy combs her wayward whiskers,
Combing them with pussy pawses.
Puss well pleased with pussy whiskers,
White and wiry; pussy proud of.

Pussy pauses in her combing,
Hears a voice call 'Pussy Wallah,
Pussy, Pussy, here's your supper.
'Pussy Wallah,' calls her Misses,
'Pussy Wallah, leave your wallow,
'Pussy, come and eat your Whiskas.'
Whiskers twitch at scent of Whiskas;
Pussy gobbles up her supper,
Purrs her thanks to Pussy's Misses.

Pussy, plump and groomed and purring,
Now returns to pussy-wallow,
Not to wallow but to settle,
Fed and flealess, placid, peaceful,
Now to sleep, and dream of mouses.

What a life, oh! Pussy-Wallah!

F Jones

VEILED LANDSCAPE

The moon casts its spell upon the emptiness of night
The long night of deep mystery
Where the familiar becomes alien
Strange sounds the only comfort
Ended by new experience of the bird at dawn
Internal and strange away from experience
Awareness of some other performance
Revealing the pangs of emotions
New shapes new hopes old fears physical spiritual
Mists to veil all expectation
The not known yet familiar feel
A prisoner released unto new captivity
The unreachable the dawn of emotion
The new horizon the Alpha and Omega
Primitive strings that pull and tug
Designed to fulfil yet deny
To give yet to take
Halcyon the times of those who experience
Of those who believe in the reality of unreality
Thanksgiving for the dreamers
Who bring to the veiled landscape of life
The power of life seasoning for to bring much
Spice that peaks and valleys and plains shall know.

Clive Cornwall

SEA MADNESS

Occult moons ebb and flow the sea tide of my mind,
And seaweed glistens at my feet.
Rose-red the evening sky unfolds
To cast a glow upon the surging brine.
Spun cobwebs shimmer in my psychic core,
And catch each thought with silken snare.
Dim echoes of wreck-fallen ships
Now whisper from the ocean's floor.
Its secret haul the haunted sea holds fast,
Of sailors, ships and gold doubloons
Of galleons, and men of war -
The sea will hold them till the last.
As through the quiet nights I roam this beach,
And hear the ocean's soothing voice,
Yet through the empty calmness comes
A wildness just beyond my reach.
As if at any given time the sea
Could swallow me with curling wave,
And with indifference could make
Itself, itself, as one with me . . .

Anne Rolfe-Brooker

LATE AUTUMN IN WILLINGHAM WOODS

Ice had formed in ruts and puddles,
One of a few things that make
Winter beautiful. Leaves' litter,
That, this autumn, once did skitter
From their twiggly homes, meets no rake.

Colours, from amber to ruddle,
(Sheep-fleece dye), crisped in frosty nights.
Two dove-wing-hued perverse clouds
Amble over land looking ploughed
Still, with crops at ridges' heights.

Gillian Fisher

MY MOTHER (SADLY NO LONGER HERE FOR MOTHER'S DAY)

I can see her by the window
Darning my dear Dad's socks,
A picture of contentment
As she tossed her curly locks.

I can see her lovely smile
When I climbed into her bed,
Where we loved to play *'I spy'*
'You go first' she always said.

I remember the river Witham
Beside which we would walk,
I told you all my secrets -
How I enjoyed our talk.

There is not a single day
That I don't think of you,
Remembering our happy times
All the things we used to do.

Never tell a lie you said,
Always keep your word,
Listen to what people say
Don't divulge what you have heard.

Be just, be kind, be honest,
Try to be brave and strong -
Never think that it is weak
To say 'sorry' when you are wrong.

Hold your head up high my daughter
As you travel life's bumpy road -
I've done my best to guide you
Now *you* must live by *your own code.*

Esther Hawkins

STORM-BOUND IN KORMAN

Wind shrieks through the rigging,
'Swift' snatches at her mooring ropes,
Foam leaves o'er the harbour bar,
Crashing waves break on the shore,
And I can feel that howling wind
Trembling through ever spar:
White foam fingers claw
At man-stacked rocks as if to tear them down,
And fill the harbour bowl once more
With wild untethered waves rushing to the shore;
Beyond the bay the wind-whipped waves leap and dance,
As on their crests white horses prance,
With wind still howling long and loud,
I take my comfort down below,
Sip coffee 'neath the lantern's glow,
Then turn my thoughts to home,
And all the while my little craft
Shakes and shudders on the foam,
As if impatient to be free
To sail again across the waves
Beyond the open sea,
Annoyed to be imprisoned here
In storm-bound harbour safe behind the wall,
The wind shrieks through the rigging,
And she longs to head the ocean's call.

Ailsa Keen

A NEW BEGINNING

And when it is my time to die
Rail not at God, nor ask him why
Do not mourn, oh! do not weep
He, safe from harm, my soul will keep

Sing no sad song, shed no sad tear
Whilst memories live, I'll still be here -
within the world whilst in your heart
And in your life I'll stay a part

Remember me for a little while
And think of me with gentle smile
The things I've done, the things I've said
And when you do, I am not dead.

Though my body dies, my soul runs free
'Tis journey's end and I will see
Through heaven's door, the prize worth winning
No not the end but a new beginning

Patricia Harrison

NATURAL WORLD

As I ramble down along the waterside
I feel so inspired with my greyhound
Strolling at my side
By the beauty of the natural world
That surrounds me

Crocuses peeping their little heads through
Snowdrops blending with surrounding snow
Upon the ground

Clouds of grey or white are drifting across the sky
The weather always makes people sigh
A rippling stream on which the sun brightly beams

A rabbit dives into his warren
The birds twitter and tweet in the trees
Too early yet for bees
Not in time yet for the leaves
But newly born buds appear upon the trees
Spring is in the air
Nature's full of care

Joy Sharp

MINUS THE BLUES

I'm leaving the blues far behind
For life's never treated me unkind.
If I'm down I count to ten
Then I chase my thoughts back round again.
I grab my coat and woolly hat
Then kiss my love, just like that.
We hit the street how it's great to feel free.
Rather this than a shopping spree.
Then it's down the road we go,
We're heading where the long grass grows.
Those clouds look ominous it might rain,
But our little walk we'll enjoy again.
Our dog Jeffery's nearly twelve,
He's a mongrel though you never could tell.
We're enjoying our stroll we're nearly home.
Back to the wife, my love, my life, my own.

David Ashley Reddish

VILLAGE LIFE

Cardiff, the cosmopolitan capital city
Was only 8 miles away . . .
Though it might have been half a world,
And reached by intercontinental jet.
From there, roads reached up the valleys,
Shadowed by hills, claustrophobic, leading to
Hirwaun, Penywaun, Tredegar and Brynmawr
Lilting names.
Villages clung to bleak hillsides like limpets to rocks,
Peopled by ex-miners and ex-miner's families,
Their livelihood, their pits, have been killed
Year by year, all unmourned at Westminster.
Chapel survived, and the conviction
That the English were marauders,
Robbing the country of its wealth and its language . . .
A language revived by middle-class incomers.
The welcome in the hillsides was a thin veneer,
Barely covering the Nationalist resentment
That simmered.
A different language; a different religion; a different attitude
To the old histories.
It was a one-sided love affair, for Wales
Never loved me.

Ann Harrison

MRS MOP

My *Mrs Mop* is a real *big treasure*
Her frequent visits give *me* much pleasure.
We exercise our tongues and joints together
And between us do a stately measure.
Belovèd *Sir* drops her off each time
To see her safe and sound on *rime*
He always gives a grin and bears it
Then quickly turns around and *hares* it.

My *Mrs Mop* is very poorly
Six months or more it must be surely,
Since she graced my doors with visage smiling
And waved the feather duster so beguiling.
I miss her so, as round I go
And grumpily complain about the dust.
Please come back soon and help me out,
I hate this daily round, this common task.

Belovèd *Sir* came once again with *Mrs Mop* in tow
With two sticks, in pain, she hobbled to my door.
'Can I come in?' she said quite ruefully
'Welcome, mind the step,' I said, and truthfully.
We exercised our tongues right merrily
Her pain forgot in laughing memory.
Next week she goes to have the pain relieved
By doctors clever and nurses beleaguered.

'I'll be back quite soon,' she said,
'To wave the feather duster o'er your bed.'
Good luck my *Mrs Mop*
You really are a *treasure*
I hope I still am here once more to get your measure!

Eileen Marie Stupples

WINTER SCENE

There's a world of white outside my door
A picture card, a snow white floor
Snowflakes falling all around
Like diamonds sparkling on the ground
No birds around that I can see
They must be sheltering in the trees
We planted them some years ago
But at that time we didn't know
How much the birds would love to hide
Safe in their haven, warm inside.
Today I see a beauty there
A world of white for us to share.
There's a world of white that's floating down
On country roads that lead to town
And all the world is quiet and still
With snow on roofs and windowsills.
There's a world of white outside this room
So sparkling in the evening's gloom
And even in the darkening light
I found it such a lovely sight
No noisy traffic passing by
Just a winter world in a darkening sky.

Margaret Pay-Watson

WHO KNOWS

Taking each day at a time,
Hoping to live in a world without crime,
You suddenly wake up and look around
Another tragedy has just been found.

You might go to bed at night
And never wake up or die of fright
Because an earthquake has just savaged a country
And thousands of people are dead in this century.

Who knows what tomorrow will bring,
Will the sun shine bright and will there be an early spring?
When the rains came, the river banks overflow,
People's homes are flooded out and spirits are low.

Perhaps it's best we don't know about tomorrow,
It might never come, so why contemplate sorrow,
Good news is always welcome to one and all of us
And we accept it completely without any fuss.

Where do we go when we cross over that line
Will it be eternity or will it be just fine?
This is our life, we make our own destiny,
No one to blame, so is this real or fantasy?

And so come what may,
Accept each day in a humble way,
Who knows, only heaven can tell,
You make your heaven on earth or your hell.

Beryl Sylvia Rusmani

APRIL

How like my life is the season of April
With its sunshine and with its rain.
With its bright blue skies and then sudden storms.
Then sunshine once again.
April flowers all look so fresh with
Both the rain and the sun.
The blackbirds all so busy searching
For materials for their nests.
So family-rearing can begin.
Oh how I love April days,
There is just so much to delight our eyes.
Not just in April
But in all the seasons of the year.

Judy Balchin

THROUGH A WOOD

I am going through a wood full of trees
When suddenly a bush did speak to me
Just take this message to the human race
I am about to return so go with haste.

I am going through a wood full of trees
When a bush spoke again that was not on fire
Hurry up and go said it for I am not a liar
Be sure they are ready to receive me.

I am going through a wood full of trees.
When the bush that spoke suddenly disappeared
Where did it go as something else will it reappear
Who do I tell or was it a dream
The meaning yet I have not seen.

Keith L Powell

WORLDS APART

Countries are separate planets
Surrounded by the spaces of seas and skies.
Variety of language loosens the ties
And in disparate dialect, comprehension dies.
All is one, we say,
But there are so many 'alls' -
All is Africa, all is Asia, all falls
Into differing categories of land, mankind and nature.
Not one creature or feature is just like another
We are all individual islands,
Eons and mansions apart,
We communicate, but in error.
We misunderstand and our mismanagement
Leads to fear and terror of the unknown,
Which is knowable
To those who listen with the inner ear,
Perceive with the inner eye.
By and by
Space will dissolve into unified wholeness,
The now-parted 'alls' and separate beings
Will meld and mould a Heaven on Earth;
There will be the birth
Of one nation, one people, one soul.
In the culmination and co-ordination of east, west,
North, south, pole and pole.
We will ascend to an infinite whole
And live an eternal, united, purposeful role.

David W Hill

THE AWAKENING

Are you aware of the hearing sounds
The richness with which the world abounds.

The sound that greets the early morn
Birds awitter in the dawn

Burbling streams . . . the wind above.
Chink of china, chime of clock.

The secret sound, too precious to tell
Of the voice we know, calling with love.

Voices of fame and majesty,
Who make occasions history.

Give thought to those who are denied
Of these, these sounds so little prized
Until one has them not . . . at all.

Stop . . . be still and think . . .
Thank the God who gave to us
The aural sense - so marvellous.

M Rose

Our True And Faithful Friend

Over the past fourteen years our lives were more complete,
You were our shadow and companion, always at our feet.
You kept this house safe, forever on guard,
No stranger could get by you.
Yet when friends arrived you did your best to get their attention
Barking and sitting at their feet, till they gave you a mention
Waiting every teatime to get the telegraph at the gate,
The paperboy was your good friend, he really was your mate.
You followed 'Regan' wherever she went
Our setter she was your little sister and also your devoted companion
Then your legs could go no more, not even for a stroll
Although your heart was strong, the years had taken their toll
So on the thirtieth of September at eleven of the hour
We said goodbye to our dear friend his legs not one ounce of power
Just like you always stayed with us
We stayed with you right to the end
Because to know you was to love you
Our true and faithful friend.

June Jefferson

OUR NATION'S FUTURE

Teaching
Preaching
Over-reaching
Speeching
Screeching
Key stage three?
No, not me
Double free.
Lee, Dee,
Tracey, Stacey,
Sharon, Darren,
Landscape barren,
Geography?
Leading?
Reading?
Almost succeeding?
What me?
Minds set free?
Could be.
Take the mess
Find success
Who can guess!
Progress?
Yes!
Outreaching
Each to each.
Targets reaching
Teaching.

Kathleen Berg

ODE TO MARKET RASEN

Your homely look deserved an ode -
Retained well since 1905,
The main A631 through road
Is much the same for all who drive -

As broad as it will ever be,
At Willingham, past the racecourse.
It tapers later, when I see
The railway bridge's span enforce

Constriction on it. In Queen Street's
Too long goose-neck, shop-buildings hold
Flex for the coloured bulbs. What treats
They are, despite December's cold!

Gillian Fisher

TOP

Acting on such information gained by studious contemplation
Of his fellow human beings most of his grown life
He knew they all respected firmness, wanted leading, needed curtness
Came to him to discuss certain aspects of their strife

He was certainly adapted through his skill for interactive
Assimilation of the tactics used by every group
Of workers in the field he furrowed; sharing papers, sumptuous suppers
He was recognised as upwards of the most renowned

Top of field he had a leaning just to keep his boots from cleaning
By himself each day come evening - he was top of shelf
Many patients, many clients spent their money most suppliant
To them especially most compliant was Sir Top of Field

But certain of his people hated one so gloriously fated
To have fame and fortune wasted on his revered being
As at his core where theories faltered he remained just as unaltered
As the spoilt child who bolstered up his parent's dreams

Of one to top the school and nation, both he did to great ovations
And everyone who knew his station crowded in his lounge
Of trophies and of pictures plenty going back to 1920
When he died his room was empty but for all of these

And now a grateful Hall remembers him and all his many embers
Are a scholarship for members of his grand calling
His boots he cleaned alone each evening, they're a pair at
                                        Tussauds leaning
Up against a plaque that's dreaming - 'The Nation Loves His Name.'

Peter Asher

MY MOTHER

My mother is my support.
She is also my friend
I know that she would fight for me
To the bitter end.

Sometimes she makes me angry
When she treats me like I'm two.
Even though I'm grown up
That is what Mother's do.

Where would I be without her.
When problems come along.
You never appreciate your Mum
Until you leave home and she's gone.

Jenny Bosworth

GOD'S GIFT OF CREATION

As autumn fades and winter starts
The leaves from trees and bushes depart,
Mulching the earth ready for another spring
The cycle of the seasons of plants and living things.

Birds have migrated to warmer climes,
How clever they are, travelling thousands of miles
And they will be back again next year,
A welcome sight when spring once more is here.

Under the soil the bulbs are stirring
And soon the snowdrops will be appearing.
Kept warm and snug under a blanket of snow,
Whatever the weather, plants still grow.

God's wonderful creation still holds mystery
From the smallest insect to the tallest tree.
Man can make so many things we need
But only *God* gives life to the seed.

Vera Hankins

AN ALTERNATIVE JOURNEY
(Reflexology)

A gently touch here, a firmer one there
The message is picked up
Relayed along the line
To all the vital parts,
Like some intricate railway network
Spreading across the country
A point needing adjustment.
Energy, rushing like some Express
To all the extremities.
Balancing finely all the points
As the main body relaxes
At each terminal connection.
Background music
Splayed over the speakers.
Everything lulled into security
On an hour or so journey into the furthest
Corner of the system.
Completed and utter compliancy
Until the final destination, then
Returning, alighting from the seat
The journey over.
All is complete.

Polly Bennison

DUELLING REDBREASTS

Soft staring eye beaded black
Entered arena, no turning back
Guardian protector, home and nest
Blood flowing, proud crimson chest
Staining suit, feather faded brown
Twisting concentration, in flickered frown
Dancing duel, fighting freedom's fall
Answering fate's death-filled call
Short swords stabbing fatal thrust
Figures tussling, rain streaked dust
Deadly dash, song sharpened beak
Mortal solitude dying lonely seek
Victor flying red crusted shirt
Battered corpse embraces bloodied dirt.

Luke Thomas

DAYBREAK

Grass glistens with refreshing morning dew
welcoming light climbs over shadowed vale
sunrise swell, coloured tinge and hue
casting glow over farmer's collected bale

Settling shaded pattern upon stubbled field
scattered straw and chaff burnished gold
birdsong basking in filtered sunlight's shield
trapped in creeping dawn's waking hold

Lambent heat warms night-chilled soil
windblown husks drifting motes of dust
gathered harvest reflects man's honest toil
tractor's metal paused in settled rust

Daybreak's signal cracks the gloaming spell
resuming shackled cycle of harvest hell

Paul Birkitt

A Fair Foxy Kop

Was on a cold and frosty night
As I lay in my bed, with
Thoughts of hotter climates
Simmering in my head, when,

Suddenly, outside I saw a light
Triggered off by an unseen hand
Was there a perpetrator
A lurking on my land?

Who could it be at two o'clock
A skulking round my door?
I pressed my face against the window
Thought 'I'd better ring the law.'

On second thoughts I peered again
The hedges my eyes were raking
A shadow of a fox is there
His bushy brush is shaking

Outlined by light and moon
A star in his own right
He slinks off into the shadows
Deep into frosty night.

Theresa Eady

SQUARE

Drawing a sad square
On the page
Black lines punctuate the white space
Paper's like a mirror
I see my reflection and it sees me
Am I really a quadrilateral?
Do corners represent an unwillingness
To bend and break out?
Hard as a grid but soft as a cushion
I see my round face turn square
My nonchalant expression turn melancholic
Pencil depicts mouth as an arch
Water runs over the bridge
And drips underneath it, into it
The saturated bridge crumbles
Like the page
The square feels the force of the rubber
But it won't rub out

W E Deweltz

A MAN WITH DOG AND STICK

To city dweller, thrashed by urban noise and crowds
Where concrete towers and blocks incarcerate,
The changing-coloured moors become escape,
And only in their vastness can he contemplate
The timelessness of time. They are to him
Synonymous with his need for solitude.
Out of this world he finds himself withdrawn
And here discovers his beatitude.
His trusted friends are near,
For company and for stance -
His stick to help him cross the rugged sheen;
His dog at heel with comprehending glance,
Having each a share of blessed tranquillity,
    Can this be immortality?

Bernard Wright

ONE LAST LOOK

Standing all alone and derelict on the edge of these windswept moors.
Is a house with many memories which has survived two World Wars.
Its roof is partly missing having blown away in a gale,
Where it faced all kinds of weather such as snow, rain and hail.
A wooden gate with broken hinges keeps swinging to and fro,
While the garden's like a jungle as the nettles and weeds will show.
There's no glass in any windows while the front door just creaks
                        and whines.
As rambling roses grew on the outside walls along with those
                        twisting vines.
Smelling damp and rather musty as you take a peek inside,
With dust just lying everywhere whilst the cobwebs dangle with pride.
The stairs are still accessible, the banister is splintered and worn,
A book has been left on the landing with pages that are torn.
Entering each of the bedrooms where they look so cold and bare.
One in particular I remember as I used to sleep in there.
Pretty curtains were hung in the windows and dolls on the bed
                        there would be
As I sat and did my homework until it was time for tea.
This house will always be special, it was home to my mum, dad and me.
Now I must leave it one last time, as they are demolishing it at three.

Jennifer Withers

WWW

Double-u, double-u, double-u dot.
I'm sick of the sound of this Internet rot!
It's changing our world, and here's a surprise
'Com's are now dotted instead of the i's!
It's forward slash this and forward slash that
'Log onto our website. Give us your cash!'
Shopping on laptops, it won't take a mo.
Tap in your order and give it a go!
Grasping the nettle I tried to log on
And accessed a site, when something went wrong.
A virus appeared and ate up my drive
My PC was dead. It didn't survive.
You try to take part and what have you got?
Double-u, double-u, double-u dot.

Andrew Mackie

SECRET SECRETS

Secrets are words, not to give away,
Secrets are words, one should not say,
Secrets can be said upon one's star,
Secrets can be kept,
If they are in one's heart.

Jessie Burke

STORMING OFF

Could the storming rain,
ease the pain,
of a turbulent mind.
And the sound of pacing feet,
give thought a beat,
clarity to find.
But emotions tossed,
like the raging winds,
settle slowly.
And calmness with exhaustion calls,
ending the squall.

Nicola Grant

THE BREAKDOWN

In the corner of an empty room
I sit hunched, arms around knees
The walls are plain and dull
emptiness reverberates between.
Where am I? Perhaps inside my mind
As I shut out the dull hum of suburbia,
the cacophony of routine,
the symphony of similarity.

Is there no door, no exit or escape?

My strength seems to ebb, my concentration goes.

Who am I?
A mother? A wife?
My heart tries to scream -
I'm a person, I am me!
But that me seems lost, so hidden in the depths; unable to be seen.
When did it leave me? I know the exact day.
It crept up slowly, but in an instant
took the person me away.

Diane Webb

TO DIANA

Diana of the bow that's worn
In memory of those who died
Of AIDs, from Kensington, or else
From Northants' flowery island, come,

Who blushed when Actaeon's cameras snapped
Your body in a Gallic cave,
And now his hounds still gnaw your ghost
In documentary poetry,

Come and tell what it is like
To die, to lie lovelorn with death,
Still chaste, and join Calcutta's nun,
Living on or just asleep,

A country's undiscovered dreams.
Come and tell my stubborn man,
Born of Bournemouth crags or lions,
No more to ignore my plea,

But bury me beneath his breast.

Jon Trenchard

In Coldness Shine

Pockets dwell
in snowy waste;
particles of dew
in frozen mist.

Stalagmites that grace
in caverns cover
the rocky face;
as ships steer
through the flotsam
to catch tundra's spring.

Fish that swim
in splits of ice;
flowers that thrust
from fissures so deep.

Hillsides that climb
as green is exposed.
Limbs that regrow
on tree's shorn so bare;
cracks reappear
in life-force reborn.

Geoffrey Ellis Fitzjohn

OUTSIDE OF TOWN

In a lovely little wood,
A little tumble-down cottage stood.
Roses still grow around the door,
An old carpet still lays on the floor.
But the cottage is not alone,
Lots of things make it a home.
Under the floor is the home of a mouse,
That is what she calls her house.
A spider weaved her web as a net,
To catch all the flies she can get.
Fungi grows up the wall,
Ants and beetles pay it a call.
Plenty of fruit, nuts and seed from the trees.
Fall with a gale or gentle breeze.
Something else will make a racket,
An owl and bats live in the attic.
For everything there is plenty of shelter,
Squirrels and bats sleep in the winter.
So although the cottage is tumbling down,
She is the happiest cottage outside of town.

Margaret Upson

MOTHER

We suckled on your breast
Life given and sustained.
Sheltered and warm,
Safe in your love.

We held your fingers
Gently pushed into the world.
Gaining confidence,
Enough to let go.

Knowing you are there
And there is home.
We stride on unafraid.
Guided by your shining light.

We journey onward
Life comes with its conditions.
Building a place takes time
But you are there,
And there is home.

Time ticks on
One year, then ten.
Life plays its game with us.
A promise of eternity . . . broken.

We sit at your bedside.
Life ending. 'Don't go!'
Exposed and so cold.
Yet still safe in your love.

Roger A Carpenter

REFLECTIONS ON AN ENGLISH COUNTY

Dorset, just one of England's lovely counties,
No endless moors or mountains high
Yet created by nature to please the eye.

A coast that stretches for many miles
With seaside fun to bring laughter and smiles,
Rambling on hills or grand coastal walks,
Or just gazing to sea, subduing all talk.

From Swanage town with its delicate charms
Walk Purbeck Hills across Nine Barrows Down,
The turf on the Down will welcome the leather
And Corfe at the end, you'll remember forever.

Dorset, not just a country's wonderful playground
But a vital live area of which we are proud
With towns of grace and quaintly named villages,
Portrayed by Hardy as 'Far from the madding crowd'.

Dorset, my preferred and favourite county,
Its narrow, wooded lanes bordered with flowers
And rippling streams, to add to nature's bounty;
Better by far than man-made summer bowers.

Age for me, has now taken a well tracked toll,
I would again that I could walk the hills and commons,
See once more the sun, set on a coastal view,
Knowing tomorrow would bring fresh strength to start anew.

Edgar Wall

A PERFECT MOMENT

A perfect moment
there can be.
A perfect moment
For you
For me
The view of mountains
The roar of the sea.
The yellow in a flower,
Your eye-catching sight
Of me.

J Campbell

EASTER SPRINGTIME...

Our flowers of spring,
bring love within, our heart,
The blossoms of Easter,
sent from our Lord
touches every tree.
From the very start,
the voice of love,
and fragrance of roses,
entwines our dreams.
He then sends us the sunlight,
which dances on the streams.
As in Heaven,
we must pray to Him for everything,
to us, He has given . . .

John A Shaw

DIVINE FORGIVENESS

The old woman sitting hunched in a shabby silent room,
The last of the evening's light coming feebly through a
window behind her chair, was barely visible in the gloom.
A tattered relic that must have been salvaged from her past.
She did not turn to look at the man as he entered the room,
the screen door, clattering behind, closing fast.

Her complexion, the colour of unrefined sugar, the end result
of generations of racial mixture, sunken in her face with high
cheek bones, a patrician nose and generous mouth.

Surely, she must have been a beautiful woman at one time in
her turbulent life.
The body slumped in the rickety chair seemed frail and brittle
but her eyes like ripe olives, jet black, studying the stranger,
were dead.

Oh Mother, after all these years, I find you in dire straits,
See, I am your son!
Why, oh why, did you forsake me when so young?
I care not for the colour of my skin, a racial prejudice we
could not win.
Rich blood from white and brown runs warmly through my veins
this mixture I do not abhor.
My heartbeat is strong and nurtures love for you.
My soul is cleansed of evil and to Heaven one day it will soar.

The light had almost gone now, the room succumbing to the
onslaught of dusk, the night air reeking of disease and pain.
Sobs reverberated into that sparsely furnished room like the
moans of a wounded animal deep in a secret jungle glade, where
nothing else might hurt or maim.

Only the opulent moon bore witness to the sorrow within.
And, love entered the heart of man and woman with all the heart
lurching suddenness of a lightning flash at midnight.

My son, I ask for a little more, your love I need before it is
too late and your forgiveness for my sins.

Dorothy F White

ISLAY

I'm looking out the window
and the beauty I can see
it surpasses anything I have seen
when I've travelled across the seas

I've been to many countries
and wonders I have seen
but back home here on Islay
the scenery is supreme

I know I wasn't born here
but I think of it as home
for when I settled down in life
it was where I made my home

So no matter to which country
my footsteps they will take
when tired of all my travelling
'Islay' my resting place I'll make

Sandra McKinnon

SHINING STAR

Shining star, shining bright
lighting up the darkest night.
Shining star, showing the way
to where the little baby lay.
In a manger fast asleep,
not a sound, not a peep.
I stood and looked at the straw that's rough
and I knew it was baby Jesus.

J Cross

EVACUEE

We had to travel to the country,
Dark and dismal and green,
The train was bumpy and uncomfortable,
The worst place we'd ever seen.
The littlest children were sobbing,
And the older ones were sad,
We didn't think it was fair,
The war was making us mad.
Clutching to our cases.
We got off the train,
And then the worst thing happened;
It began to rain.
We had to walk right to the school,
Everyone sopping wet,
We took our dripping clothes off,
Then the teacher was to be met.
We wrote a postcard to our Mums,
Telling her we had arrived,
Then we posted it at the Post Office
Can't we come home now?

Kirsty Hewitt (10)

SIGHTINGS FROM COMFORT

I gazed the skies on a field one night
hoping to catch, a UFO in my sight
when a bat flew over, shrieking in high pitch
my telescope fell down, into a ditch.

I tumbled in the dark, to find the telescope,
lost my footing, and rolled down the slope.
Up to my knees, in water and grasses
couldn't see a thing, for all the dirt on my glasses.

Slipping and sliding, starting to loose hope
as trying to climb up the muddy slope.
It was thanks to lightning, which lit up the ground,
for my water filled telescope, was to be found.

Wet, cold, tired and covered in mud
I cursed my misfortune, and rotten luck.
It was cloudy now, raining and late
the only sound I heard, was a frog, serenading his mate.

Feeling frozen I hurried home, first walking, then I ran,
to find a note on the table, from the old man.
He'd seen strange lights, from the comfort of his armchair,
while I was paddling in mud, in cold and wet . . . way out there!

Satu Browne-Pennanen

REFLECTIONS

I gaze into the mirror,
she glares back in my eyes.
I want to call it trickery
and say it's only lies.
I fix my gaze so steadily
and ask can it be me.
I seem to look much younger,
how can it really be?

Those eyes are brown and knowing,
I've had them all my life,
but where have all the wrinkles gone?
Could it be the surgeon's knife?
My nose is slightly smaller,
my face is almost round.
But as I go on looking
I know it's me I've found.

The mirror's looking misty,
I give a little grin -
how can I look so beautiful,
it, surely is a sin.
I've lived to almost 50,
and worn like all the rest.
I've had a worried life.
Why? Do I look my best?

My gaze now finds reality.
Why should the mirror falter?
Because it's just a windowpane
And I'm looking at my daughter.

Alexandria Phipps

I'M OFF DAD

I'm off to fight a war Dad
Our country's calling me
They'll be sending me to France Dad
or maybe Italy
The Army is my first choice
I hope to do quite well
But pray for me at night Dad
for War's a living hell
My stomach keeps on churning
with fear deep down inside
A feeling of foreboding and
nowhere now to hide
Though with your strength and guidance
which helped me through the years
I will withstand all traumas
and dissipate all fears
Farewell to you for now Dad
say goodbye to Mum
No matter what the outcome
Your ever loving son.

Dusty S

BIRTHDAYS

The birthday boy or girl is always present.
Presents and kisses are greatly received.
Celebrated by parties with family
They can also be celebrated with friends.
Birthdays are for having fun with your friends.
Sausage rolls, cakes and jelly for all to enjoy.
Cards are given sometimes including money.
Birthstones, birth flowers and zodiac sign represent
The twelve months of the year you are born in.
January through to December are the months.
Surprises galore are in store for you.
Trips out to places you have never been.
These can be with family or your friends.
On your 100th you receive a letter from the Queen.

Keith Clarke (13)

Out Of Life

I lay on my worn, cold, empty bed to sleep,
Closing my eyes shut but feeling that they're open.
My worries and fears float around in my mind,
I can't get no needed sleep but still I try.
First dark circles appear under my tired eyes,
Followed by loss of appetite and loss of mind.
Soon I'm certain I will run out of energy,
My body will no longer run at its normal pace.
What will it take to get me away from this,
Shall I ever battle my way through.
Pounding headaches haunt me still,
Restlessness is such a good friend of mine.
My desperate cries for help go unheard,
Always I search for that light at the end of the tunnel.
I wonder if there is another side to life,
Just wishing and picturing it within my mind.

Zoe Fitzjohn

PLANTING ACORNS

A kindly gesture means a lot when you feel sad and blue,
A friendly smile can help a lot and a cheery word or two.
Each one of us may need a friend, for a short time or for life,
For anyone depressed and sad it helps to share their strife.

A sunny smile can lighten a lonely person's day
And helps them face the world again and ease them on their way.
Who knows what this could lead to, or where your kindness goes,
For it's from a little acorn that a mighty oak can grow.

Pauline Anderson

PICTURES IN MY GARDEN

My little garden brings me joy in the winter when it's dull
The greens and silvers of the leaves glisten in the snow.
Spring warmth grows and bulbs do flower,
Bringing rainbows of colour.
Daffodils and tulips dance in the wind
Snowdrops and crocus sit still and the birds do sing.
Summer bursts with rays of sun,
Large blooms open wide so the bees can get their pollen,
Butterflies flutter on the breeze and birds sing up in the trees,
Then before I realise it bright colours turn to burnt orange and gold,
And autumn is here again
Leaves fall from the trees making a carpet on the ground,
Sun fades in the evening and the sky does turn to red,
Misty dew in the morning glistens on the spider's web
Then back into wintry ice and snow getting ready once again
                              for everything to grow.

Jenny Johnson

CLOCKING OFF

41 years, his last day at work
He expected some appreciation, some farewell perk.

No one wished him well, it was a depressing scene.
How could his company be so very mean?

No fond farewells, nothing to say.
He just walked away like a normal day.

Sad and depressing he walked every familiar street.
A young female neighbour stopped him, who he'd occasionally meet.

He told her his sad tale, she sympathised with his plea.
Inviting him in for a welcome cup of tea.

She warmed to his problems, she made him feel fine.
After their tea they went on to the wine.

The warmth of her presence made him feel great.
She said she could comfort him, if it was not too late.

She said, 'Give me ten minutes, I will get rid of your gloom.
I am going to get comfortable in the next room.'

Soon she would put his eager body to the full test.
So he stripped off his clothes right down to his vest.

No longer depressed he was weathering the storm.
Ready and eager now to perform.

She called out, 'I am ready,' his heart started to soar.
Flushed with his mission, he made for the door.

He strode into the room, full of elation.
His boss and twenty colleagues were there for a presentation.

He grabbed at the gift to try to cover his shock.
There are only so many things you can do with a clock.

T Napper